THE DAYTONA 500

THE THRILL AND THUNDER OF THE GREAT AMERICAN RACE

NANCY ROE PIMM

Ⅿ MILLBROOK PRESS · MINNEAPOLIS

Author's Acknowledgments

I owe a great big thank-you to three special men that let me barge in on their "Mancation" so I could research this book— my father-in-law, George Pimm; my brother-in-law Sam Phelps; and my wonderful husband, Ed Pimm. Not only did they share their vacation with me, but they shared their knowledge and passion for stock car racing. This book would not be possible without the generosity of our longtime friend, Chip Ganassi, who opened the doors of his fine racing establishment, and special thanks to John Olguin for always looking out for me. Thanks John Andretti for being the great guy you are, plus a wonderful racer and writer! Thanks to historian Eddie Roche for taking the time to check the manuscript for historical accuracy. Thanks to Loren Scully, Mary Viscuso, and Ray Barrett of the Dublin, Ohio, library for all of your help with books and research. Thanks always to my critique buddies Erin MacLellan, Margaret Peterson Haddix, Jenny Patton, Linda Stanek, and Linda Gerber. Many thanks to Tanya Dean for beginning this journey with me and for always believing in me. Thanks to the many mechanics and engineers, such as Jimmy Elledge, Tim Smith, Tony Glover, Tony Santanicola, and Ray Fox, who shared their knowledge and expertise. Special thanks to the drivers, especially Richard Petty, Bobby Allison, Morgan Shephard, Paul Goldsmith, and Jamie McMurray for taking the time for personal interviews. And last, but not least, thanks to my editor, Matt Doeden, for your vision and focus and for asking the question, "Who named it the Great American Race?" Congrats to Chip Ganassi on winning the trifecta of auto racing in 2010: the Indy 500, the Brickyard 400, and the Daytona 500.

Text copyright © 2011 by Nancy Roe Pimm

Millbrook Press
A division of Lerner Publishing Group, Inc.
241 First Avenue North
Minneapolis, MN 55401 U.S.A.

Website address: www.lernerbooks.com

Library of Congress Cataloging-in-Publication Data

Pimm, Nancy Roe.
    The Daytona 500 : the thrill and thunder of the great American race / by Nancy Roe Pimm.
      p.   cm. — (Spectacular sports)
    Includes bibliographical references and index.
    ISBN 978–0–7613–6677–5 (lib. bdg. : alk. paper)
    1. Daytona 500 (Automobile race)—History—Juvenile literature. 2. Stock car racing—United States—History—Juvenile literature. I. Title.
GV1033.5.D39P55 2011
796.720975921—dc22   2010027263

Manufactured in the United States of America
1 – DP – 12/31/10

Contents

Introduction: Fasten Your Seat Belts 5

1 The Birthplace of Speed 7

2 The Early Years of Daytona 14

3 Recent Decades 25

4 The Cars, Inside and Out 34

5 Start Your Engines! 43

Special Feature: Behind the Wheel with John Andretti 54

Flags of NASCAR 57

NASCAR Glossary and Slang 58

Source Notes 61

Further Reading 62

Index 63

Fans pack the grandstand in Daytona Beach, Florida, to watch the cars roar by at the start of the 2009 Daytona 500.

Introduction:
FASTEN YOUR SEAT BELTS

What takes two months of preparation, two weeks of practice, and two laps of qualifying? It's the Daytona 500, the Super Bowl of the National Association for Stock Car Auto Racing (NASCAR) circuit. While most major sports end their season with a bang, NASCAR kicks off its season with a 500-mile explosion called the Great American Race. About 200,000 eager race fans travel to the Daytona tri-oval each February to cheer on their favorite drivers. The two weeks of practicing, qualifying, and racing is called Speedweeks, with a capital *S*!

NASCAR drivers work their way up through many different roads to reach the pinnacle of their career, the Daytona 500. Some circle dirt-covered tracks, others negotiate the twists and turns of road racing, while still others compete in go-karts. They are all weekend warriors, traveling from track to track. Most drivers win championships in one series or another on their journey to the Sprint Cup Series and the Daytona 500.

Some drivers believe that winning the Daytona 500 is better than winning a championship. "You can't call your career complete unless you put a Daytona win under your belt," said former champ Mario Andretti. "And you only get one chance a year. It's almost unfair."

"It's the ultimate race," said three-time Daytona 500 winner Jeff Gordon following his 2005 Daytona 500 victory. "There's just no better place to win at than Daytona. You know the sport's getting more competitive. It's getting bigger and it's just one of those races if you pick one, this is the one you want to win."

Race car drivers get ready to race across the sands of Daytona Beach in 1925.

1 The Birthplace of Speed

The year was 1903. America's roads were courses for horses, not cars. NASCAR wouldn't exist for another 44 years. Automotive pioneer Ransom E. Olds was vacationing at Ormond Beach, Florida, when he discovered that the long coastline and the hard-packed beaches of Daytona and Ormond were ideal for high-speed driving. The damp sand cooled a car's tires, maximizing grip. And cars didn't kick up clouds of dust as they did on dirt roads.

On March 28, a match race between Ransom Olds and wealthy car owner Alex Winton was the talk of the town. H. T. Thomas, an Oldsmobile engineer, drove Ransom Olds's car. It was nicknamed the *Pirate* for its bare-bones appearance. Alex Winton drove his own car, which he called the *Bullet*. The Ormond Challenge Cup was to be the first official race on the beach.

Once the dead fish and other sea debris were cleared from a one-mile stretch of sand, the beach course was ready. At the pop of the gun, H. T. Thomas stomped on the gas. His car reached speeds of nearly 50 miles per hour. Slow off the line, Winton was about 50 yards behind before he even got going. But at the finish, the *Bullet* shot by the *Pirate*, winning by about one-fifth of a second.

Tragedy in Daytona

The deaths of 27-year-old Frank Croker and his mechanic Alexander Raoul overshadowed the Winter Speed Carnival of 1905. Croker, a car owner but not a professional driver, swerved into the surf when a motorcycle suddenly veered into his path. The accident showed the danger of letting amateur drivers take part in the races. Since then, most car owners have hired professional drivers to race their cars.

The lure of being the fastest racer in the land attracted many drivers. Soon racers from all over the world flocked to Daytona Beach to shatter speed records. From 1903 to 1910, the races on the beach were called the Winter Speed Carnival. By 1910 there was an official Speedweek in February at Daytona. The beaches of Ormond and Daytona became known as the birthplace of speed.

The British Are Coming

Daytona wasn't just about racing. It was also about setting records. In 1927 British racer Henry Segrave came to Daytona Beach to make his mark in the record books. Known as the Mad Major, he drove the *Golden Arrow*, a 1,000-horsepower vehicle propelled by two V-12 airplane engines. Segrave's speed of 203 miles per hour made him the first driver to exceed the 200 miles per hour mark.

Henry Segrave sits in his specially designed race car, the *Golden Arrow*.

Airflow features on the *Bluebird (racing on the sand)* were not found in automobiles until decades later. The high stabilization fin was later copied in speedboats. Modern 707 jets have air flaps similar to the ones used on the *Bluebird*.

A year later, rival and fellow Brit Sir Malcolm Campbell broke the speed record in a car he called the *Bluebird*. Over the years, the two drivers went back and forth, swapping records. To be official, the speed records had to be run in two stages. The stages were run in opposite directions, one mile up and one mile back. The speed of the two runs was then averaged to tally the official speed record. This ensured that wind was not a factor.

On March 5, 1935, Campbell arrived from Britain. He brought a team of mechanics and his latest version of the *Bluebird*. The 28-foot teal-colored car weighed just less than five tons. It was fitted with air flaps and fins. It was powered by a 1,343-cubic-inch (22-liter) Rolls Royce aircraft engine that produced 2,500 horsepower. Two days later, Campbell and the *Bluebird* reached a speed of 330 miles per hour. The tires blistered, sending Campbell into a slide. After regaining control of his vehicle, he crossed the finish line with an average speed of 276.82 miles per hour.

Clearly high speeds and the beach's sandy surface were a dangerous combination. Campbell's attempt was the last such recorded speed run at Daytona.

Thunder on the Beach

The city of Daytona was determined to keep race fans coming back each year. The city connected the beach course to the narrow two-lane blacktop of Highway A1A, creating a 3.2-mile oval racetrack. Cars could race side by side on this beast of a track—half-sand, half-asphalt.

The first National Championship Beach and Road Race was held on March 6, 1936. The racers faced unique challenges in the 250-mile race. Changing from sand to asphalt and back again caused cars to spin and fishtail (lose grip with the rear tires). Windshields were coated with wet sand. Highway A1A, barely wide enough for two cars, made passing an adventure. Then the tide came in, and the race was stopped.

"Big Bill" France moved to Daytona Beach, Florida, from Washington, D.C., in 1935. As a teenager, Bill used to skip school to race at a track in Maryland.

The auto race had been a disaster. Daytona turned to motorcycles, which were better suited for the sandy course. About 20,000 fans turned out for the first motorcycle race.

Big Bill's Vision

Automobile racing at Daytona might have ended if it hadn't been for the fifth-place finisher of the National Championship Beach and Road Race, "Big Bill" France. France convinced a local club to support another auto race in 1937. Auto racing at an improved beach course resumed until 1941. It stopped during World War II (1941–1945), then resumed in 1947. Drivers came for the Grand National races, which were held on a newly lengthened 4.1-mile course.

Cars kick up clouds of sand as they round a turn on Daytona Beach in 1940. Atlantic Ocean waves pound the coast while race spectators look on.

Big Bill had a vision. He wanted to start an organization to govern stock car racing. It would provide a clear set of rules, a solid schedule of events, and a national championship based on points earned at each race. The cars were to be "strictly stock," affordable, and free of dents. They were called stock, meaning "standard or typical." Stock cars were not specially built just for racing. Racers could drive their family car right from the road onto the track. Fans could root for the makes and models of cars they themselves drove.

Monday Payday

Car manufacturers saw the value in having their cars win races. Because most races took place on Sundays, they had a saying: "What wins on Sunday, sells on Monday!"

The Birth of NASCAR

On December 14, 1947, France gathered about 35 drivers, mechanics, and businesspeople at the Streamline Hotel in Daytona Beach. He spoke of making stock cars affordable and simple, so that the driver, rather than the car, would stand out. France reasoned that this idea would attract more competitors and more fans. A point system was jotted down on a napkin. Those gathered even agreed to rules such as "All cars must be brightly painted." Mechanic Red Vogt suggested naming the new organization the National Association for Stock Car Auto Racing. NASCAR was born!

In this 1948 race, cars hit the paved portion of the Daytona Beach track.

NASCAR rules allowed drivers to make only minor changes to their cars. They taped up or removed the headlights for safety. They strapped leather belts around the door frames to keep the doors from flying open. They removed mufflers, rear seat cushions, and wheel covers to make the cars lighter and faster. Some drivers concocted heavy-duty seat belts from the military surplus stores. Others used old horse harnesses or simply took the belts off their pants to strap themselves in. Drivers didn't wear all the protective gear they wear today. Helmets and goggles were the only protective gear required. Drivers often just slapped numbers on the sides of their cars, and it was off to the races.

NASCAR legend Richard Petty remembers traveling to the races with his family as a young boy. "My dad and myself, my mom and my brother, would get in the family car to go to the races," he said. "On the way, we would stop at a Texaco station to put the car up on the rack. We changed the oil, checked the tire pressures, took the mufflers off, took the hubcaps off, and put a number on, and all of a sudden it was a race car."

The First Roll Cage

In 1953 Lee Petty reinforced his roof with pipe to prevent it from collapsing if the car rolled over. NASCAR officials said that there was nothing in the rule book about roll bars. But Petty argued that it was a safety issue. NASCAR agreed to allow the roll cage and list it in the rule book. Roll bars, along with the shoulder harness, became standard equipment in the 1960s.

"There is no doubt about the date people began racing automobiles. It was the day they built the second automobile."

—Richard Petty

2 The Early Years of Daytona

The city of Daytona grew. Attendance at the stock car races increased. By 1954 three new homes had been built in the middle of the racecourse. Their driveways led right to the track! Daytona needed a permanent racetrack with ample seating. It was time to leave the beach behind.

On November 25, 1957, crews began clearing ground for Daytona Beach International Speedway, a 480-acre motor sports complex. With the backing of supporters, Bill France built a 2.5-mile track with 31-degree banking (slope from the inside part of the track to the outside part).

Seven garages with enough space for 162 cars were built on the infield. Seating for more than 100,000 fans was added. Earthmovers took away dirt from the infield to build the banked turns and created a 44-acre rectangular lake. They called it Lake Lloyd, after Saxton Lloyd, a local businessman who supported the track.

The shape of the track was neither a circle nor an oval. It was a D-shaped tri-oval. Drivers didn't even have to use their brakes on the track's banked corners. The track measured 40 feet wide, all of which could be used for racing. The 3,000-foot-long backstretch was straight and banked only enough for water drainage. The turns at the end of the track were 3,000 feet as well. The track was so big that rain could be falling at one corner of the tri-oval while the other was dry.

"There have been other tracks that separated the men from the boys," noted Jimmy Thompson, who finished 20th in the first Daytona 500. "This is the track that will separate the brave from the weak after the boys are gone."

The final race on the beach, won by Paul Goldsmith, was held on February 23, 1958. The stage was set for the first Great American Race. The tradition of exciting Daytona 500 finishes was about to begin.

Construction workers make one of the banked portions of the Daytona Beach International Speedway in 1958.

What's in a Name?

The Daytona 500 wasn't called the Great American Race until 1982. Race announcer Ken Squier was thinking about how the Indianapolis 500 (the most famous race in U.S. Indy car racing) was called the Greatest Spectacle in Racing and how the Daytona 500 didn't have a nickname of its own. After Bobby Allison's 1982 Daytona 500 victory, Squier dubbed it the Great American Race.

PHOTO FINISH

The first Daytona 500, held in February of 1959, gave the fans a lot to talk about. None of the 59 drivers who competed in the event knew what to expect. "We all went in there blind," said Richard Petty.

Petty remembers that for the first practice the drivers were told to stay off the banking of the racetrack for the first five laps. After one and a half laps, 21-year-old Petty couldn't wait any longer. He drove up onto the banking. When he crossed the start/finish line, he found the black flag waving. The black flag is NASCAR's way of warning a driver who is breaking a rule. This made Richard Petty the first man to be black-flagged in the history of the Daytona 500.

The race itself featured 33 lead changes. It was accident free, without a single caution period (laps in which the field is slowed down because of an accident or dangerous condition). On the final lap, race leaders Lee Petty and Johnny Beauchamp came upon the slower, lapped car (a car that is a full lap behind the leader) of Joe Weatherly. Beauchamp went low on the track. Petty was sandwiched between Weatherly and Beauchamp. Together, the three cars streaked across the finish line. Officials agreed that Beauchamp was the winner. Beauchamp took his No. 73 T-Bird to the grassy infield to accept the trophy. Meanwhile, Petty and his fans argued that he was the winner. Although Petty left the track without the prize money, he felt confident. "I'm sleeping good because I know I had Beauchamp beat by about two feet," he said.

Track officials waited for newsreel footage of the finish before paying out the prize money. About 61 hours after the checkered flag signaled the end of the first Daytona 500, Lee Petty was declared the winner. He was awarded the trophy and a purse of $19,050. Embarrassed by the turn of events, France decided there was no way he would be put in such a difficult position again. "This is the first time so close a finish has ever occurred in auto racing," he said. "We won't be caught off guard again. We'll install a photo finish camera on the line."

Lee Petty (No. 42) noses out Johnny Beauchamp (No. 73) for the win in the 1959 Daytona 500. The third car (No. 48) is Joe Weatherly's, who is one full lap behind.

CINDERELLA STORY

FEBRUARY 24, 1963

At the American Challenge Cup on February 14, 1963, a Maserati tumbled down the Daytona racetrack end over end and slid to a stop on its roof. Flames erupted inside and outside the mangled car, trapping driver Marvin Panch. Driver DeWayne "Tiny" Lund was watching the race. The 270-pound Lund was one of several onlookers to rush to the flaming car. He grabbed a fire extinguisher, stuck it into the cockpit, and started spraying. Then he pulled Panch to safety.

Panch was badly burned. He could not drive in the Daytona 500, which was to be held ten days later. He and his car owners, Glen and Leonard Wood, decided to offer Lund the chance to be his replacement. Lund was an experienced driver, but he had never won at the highest level.

Marvin Panch is shown with his No. 21 Maserati before the February 1963 race that left him badly burned.

He had come to the Daytona 500 just hoping to work on someone's crew for the race. Instead, he was offered the chance to drive for one of the best teams in the sport!

It was the race of Lund's life. Late in the race, he was trailing Fred Lorenzen and Ned Jarrett. With eight laps to go, Lorenzen had to pit (stop) for fuel. Jarrett took over the lead. But one lap later, Jarrett had to pit as well. That gave Lund a big lead. The only question was whether he had enough fuel. Lund kept going and going, lap after lap. He finally ran out of fuel in the final turn. But he coasted to the checkered flag. Against all odds, he had won the Great American Race!

After the race, Lund said, "I wanted to win for Marvin and the Wood Brothers because they took a chance." The Wood brothers must have liked to take chances, because not only did Tiny Lund win the race but he won it on a single set of tires, which was very rare. When asked what he planned to do with the prize money, Lund smiled and said, "I'm going to pay my bills."

DeWayne "Tiny" Lund is all smiles as he holds his wife in one arm and the winner's trophy in the other.

SUPER MARIO

FEBRUARY 16, 1967

Mario Andretti is the only driver who can boast a hat trick by winning the Daytona 500, the Indianapolis 500, and the Formula One championship. Andretti was a rookie at the 1967 Daytona 500. He used an unusual style, riding the bottom of the track around the turns and letting the car drift up to the wall. He left his back end hanging out, meaning that the rear tires were only loosely gripping the track.

This style gave Andretti great speed, but that speed came at a risk. If the rear tires lost any more grip, the car could spin out. This thrilled the fans and unnerved the other drivers. Many drivers expected that Andretti wouldn't even make it to the finish line. But they were wrong. Andretti didn't just make it to the checkered flag, he won the race!

Top: Mario Andretti drives the No. 11 car to the high side of the track in the 1967 Daytona 500. *Bottom:* Mario Andretti and his wife Dee Ann celebrate with fans and reporters after the race.

LAST-LAP RIVALRY

FEBRUARY 15, 1976

In the early years, the Daytona had no radio communication, no television monitors, no computers, and no instant replay. But winning at Daytona is never simple. Richard Petty and David Pearson battled during the last lap of the 1976 Daytona 500. The matchup of the King (Petty) vs. the Silver Fox (Pearson) was one of the fiercest rivalries the sport has known.

The crowd was on their feet for the last lap. Pearson shot by Petty on the backstretch. The two cars came through the fourth turn side by side. Petty rode on along the bottom and began to pass Pearson. But before he could complete the pass, his car drifted up toward Pearson's car in the high lane. Pearson didn't budge. Petty's right rear hit Pearson's left front. Both cars slammed into the wall and came to rest on the front stretch grass.

Smoke billows from the cars of David Pearson (No. 21) and Richard Petty (No. 43) in the 1976 Daytona 500.

Bobby Allison grabs Yarlborough's foot after the last-lap crash that took brother Donnie *(left)* out of the 1979 Daytona 500.

Richard Petty saw his chance. He took the low line and kept Darrell Waltrip behind him long enough to take the checkered flag and his sixth Daytona 500 victory. But all eyes were on the crashed cars. An angry Yarborough hopped out of his car, pointing and shouting at Allison. Bobby Allison, who was also in the race, drove up to check on his brother. Yarborough whacked Bobby with his helmet. Donnie grabbed Yarborough, holding him back. The brothers wrestled him to the ground. Race officials rushed in and broke up the fight, but the replay of the incident was shown over and over again.

Rising Star

The 1979 race was the first Daytona 500 for one of the most famous drivers, Dale Earnhardt. When he nosed his way into the lead on lap 44 of his first race, the announcer said, "Earnhardt! Now there's the kid to watch!" Earnhardt led a total of 10 laps in the race before finishing eighth.

3 *Recent Decades*

The publicity generated from the wild 1979 finish brought countless new fans to stock car racing. NASCAR became a truly national sport. The spectacular show—from the wheel-to-wheel racing to the trackside brawl—left the fans wanting more.

And more they got! The sport kept growing, and the speeds kept climbing. In 1982 Benny Parsons amazed all when he became the first driver to exceed the 200 miles per hour mark in qualifying. Four years later, Bill Elliott posted a blistering qualifying speed of just over 210 miles per hour and went on to win the 1987 Daytona 500.

Bill Elliott leads the pack at the start of the 1987 Daytona 500. Elliott earned the first starting position for the race with a speed of 210 miles per hour.

50 Years

In 2008 the Great American Race celebrated 50 action-packed years. The 50th anniversary race was the first Daytona 500 for NASCAR's Car of Tomorrow (COT), which was introduced in 2007. To commemorate the event, the Harley J. Earl Daytona 500 Trophy, which goes to the winner of the race, was gold-plated instead of silver. Previous Daytona 500 champions were invited to share in the celebration of speed. Richard Petty waved the green flag *(below)*, while Junior Johnson drove the pace car.

For the safety of the fans and the drivers, NASCAR enforced a new rule in 1988 to use restrictor plates at superspeedways. The plates limit airflow into the engines, reducing horsepower—and speed.

FAMILY AFFAIR

FEBRUARY 14, 1988

For members of the Allison family, the 1988 Daytona 500 was a dream come true. After a pit stop on lap 164 of the 200-lap race, Bobby and his son Davey Allison were running in second and third place, respectively, behind Darrell Waltrip. They worked together to reel in the leader.

Following a caution, the race was restarted on lap 183. Soon after, Waltrip's car fell out of the race with mechanical problems, leaving the Allisons in the top two spots. On the final laps, two-time winner Bobby Allison checked his mirror. Davey's white and black No. 28 car continued to challenge. Taking the third turn for the final lap, Davey pulled to the inside but didn't have the speed to pass his father. He tucked in and followed his dad across the finish line.

In a postrace interview, Bobby Allison said, "What a thrill seeing Davey in my mirror coming through the dog-leg to the checkered flag and knowing we were going to sweep it." During the family celebration in victory lane, Davey had mixed emotions, "I had a lot of dreams when I was growing up. And one of them was battling my dad to the wire in a race. The only difference is I wanted to finish first."

In 1988 Bobby Allison (No. 12) earned his last career victory by beating his son Davey.

FINALLY!

Dale Earnhardt had won a lot of races at Daytona, but he had never won the 500. In 1998, on his 20th try, he finally won the crown jewel of stock car racing. Before the race, Earnhardt spoke with Wessa Miller, a young fan who had met him through the Make-a-Wish Foundation. When they met, Wessa gave Dale a penny and said, "I rubbed this lucky penny, and it's going to win you the Daytona 500. It's your race."

"I have had a lot of great fans and people behind me all throughout the years and I just can't thank them enough," Earnhardt later said. "All race fans are special, but a little girl like that—that's in a wheelchair—that life has not been good to, giving a penny and wishing luck, that's pretty special. . . . Inspiration is what it's all about. . . . Determination and having a never-say-die attitude—never giving up—those are the keys to achieve success. . . . I put that penny on the dashboard and it's still on the dashboard."

Dale Earnhardt takes the checkered flag to win the Daytona 500 in 1998.

Earnhardt lifts the trophy from his Daytona 500 victory.

Earnhardt did his part during the race. With less than two laps to go, he was battling Bobby Labonte and Jeremy Mayfield for the win. The three cars came up on the lapped car of Rick Mast. Earnhardt passed Mast on the outside, but Labonte was held up. Mayfield and Labonte were left battling for second place as Earnhardt cruised to the victory that had eluded him for so long.

"I cried a little bit in the race car on the way to the checkered flag," Earnhardt admitted. "Well, maybe not cried, but my eyes watered up." His long-awaited victory came on the 50th anniversary of the first NASCAR race ever run on the beach-road course of Daytona. "It was my time, I guess. I've been passed on the last lap, run out of gas, and cut a tire. . . . I don't know how we won it, but we won it."

TRIUMPH AND TRAGEDY

FEBRUARY 18, 2001

The fans came to their feet, eagerly anticipating the finish of the 2001 Daytona 500. Many cheered for the underdog, Michael Waltrip. Waltrip had started a record 462 races without a single win.

The race featured 49 lead changes among 14 drivers. But Waltrip had the lead on the final lap, with Earnhardt Jr. close behind and Earnhardt Sr. in third. Suddenly, Earnhardt Sr. lost control of his black No. 3 Chevrolet. The car crossed in front of oncoming traffic at high speed. Then it slammed into the outside wall. It was a violent crash, but all eyes were on Waltrip as he streaked beneath the checkered flag for the win. When Michael crossed the finish line, he said to himself, "This is the Daytona 500. Don't act like an idiot. It's just a race and you've won it. Cry now and have your stuff together when you get to victory lane."

Waltrip's brother, Darrell—a former 500 champion himself—was announcing the race. The win made the Waltrip brothers the first siblings to win at Daytona. Darrell choked up as he watched his little brother win, and he expressed concern for his friend Earnhardt.

Dale Earnhardt fans hold a candlelight vigil by the track after learning of Earnhardt's death during the race.

Michael Waltrip crosses the finish line at the 2001 Daytona 500. It is his first career win.

The Waltrip brothers couldn't have known that soon NASCAR fans natiowide would be crying. Rescue crews rushed out to Earnhardt's wrecked car. The driver wasn't moving. The force of the impact had snapped his neck and killed him instantly. "Today NASCAR lost its greatest driver in the history of the sport," NASCAR chairman Bill France said. "I lost a dear friend."

Daytona later erected a nine-foot bronze statue of Earnhardt holding his 1998 Daytona 500 trophy. The statue stands outside the speedway, reminding fans of one of the sport's greats.

HANS

Dale Earnhardt's death convinced NASCAR to put new safety rules into effect. A year later, the head and neck support (HANS) system became mandatory. The HANS system protects a driver's head and neck during crashes. When a speeding car comes to a sudden stop, the impact can exert more than 100 times the force of gravity. Seat belts stop the driver's body. But without restraint, the head keeps moving. This puts great strain on the neck. The HANS system restrains the driver's head on impact.

The Sweetest Day

FEBRUARY 14, 2010

The road to victory lane in the 2010 Daytona 500 became a greater challenge due to a large pothole that suddenly appeared on the exit of turn two. The race was delayed almost two and a half hours for repairs. The climactic ending came under the lights, with Jamie McMurray dashing to the finish line in front of hard-charging Dale Earnhardt Jr. Although McMurray led only two laps for the entire race, he led the most important one. There is an old saying at Daytona: you only have to lead the 200th lap!

Being crowned the 2010 Daytona 500 champion made Valentine's Day pretty sweet for newlywed McMurray. It was made even sweeter because a month before, he'd been out of a job after having been let go by his former team. "I never gave up on my goals, and I relied on the power of prayer," he said. "Never give up. You never know what life will bring you."

His determination paid off. He found a home with the Earnhardt-Ganassi race team and proved right away that he belonged.

"We passed back and forth," McMurray said of the final lap of the Daytona 500. "I took the lead for the

Jamie McMurray holds on to a slim lead over Dale Earnhardt Jr. as the cars approach the checkered flag in the 2010 Daytona 500.

final time in the backstretch. Fifty feet before the finish line on the last lap . . . I knew I had a chance of winning. You never know at a place like Daytona. It's a gamble. You have to put yourself in the right position and a lot of things have to go your way."

When asked how winning the Daytona 500 changed his life, McMurray said, "It really hasn't changed my life much. Winning the Daytona 500 doesn't change how you would treat people or how you would act towards people. I remember someone saying. 'Would you rather be remembered as a great racer or as a great human being?' I would like to be thought of as a great race car driver, but more importantly, I would like to be thought of as a great human being."

Daytona 500 Multiple Winners

Richard Petty—7 wins (1964, 1966, 1971, 1973, 1974, 1979, 1981)
Cale Yarborough—4 wins (1968, 1977, 1983, 1984)
Bobby Allison—3 wins (1978, 1982, 1988)
Dale Jarrett—3 wins (1993, 1996, 2000)
Jeff Gordon—3 wins (1997, 1999, 2005)
Bill Elliott—2 wins (1985, 1987)
Sterling Martin—2 wins (1994, 1995)
Michael Waltrip—2 wins (2001, 2003)

McMurray celebrates his win in the victory lane amid cheering fans and raining confetti.

4 The Cars, Inside and Out

The 43 race cars—Chevrolets, Fords, Toyotas, and Dodges—speed around the track at almost 200 miles per hour. The Daytona 500 is a test of endurance for the stock cars as well as the drivers. But don't be fooled by the sound of it. Although they are called stock cars, there is little "stock" about them.

Evolution of the Stock Car

When NASCAR began, stock cars were exactly like everyday passenger cars. But over the years, the cars had to be made stronger so they could run safely at the higher speeds. By the 1970s, the term *stock car* had come to identify race cars with full bodies on them (as opposed to open wheel cars, in which the body does not cover the wheels). In the 1990s, the cars evolved so drastically that they no longer resembled the production cars they represented. By the early 2000s, the only parts that remained stock were the hood, the deck lid, the roof, and the floor pan. In the late 2000s, new rules changed even that. Under the rules, all teams must run cars built to the same specifications. This new car, made to maximize safety, was called the Car of Tomorrow (COT).

Top engineers at NASCAR's Research and Development Center in Concord, North Carolina, spent seven years planning, developing, and testing the COT. It made its debut at the Bristol Motor Speedway March 25, 2007.

A NASCAR driver sits in the custom-fitted seat in the cockpit of his car. A HANS device secures his head and neck, protecting him from injury during a crash.

The new car is loaded with safety features. It has a larger cockpit. The inside of the car, or greenhouse, is wider. A double-frame railing with steel plating covers the driver's side door bars to stop the doors from caving in during crashes. Energy-absorbing material helps reduce the shock of crashes. The gas tank, also called the fuel cell, has a thicker, stronger bladder (protective covering) to reduce the threat of fire.

The COT also made racing more affordable for teams. Teams could no longer build a car that was suited to just one track. This helped to level the playing field, since teams with limited resources couldn't afford such a luxury. The rule keeps the focus on the driver, not on the car itself.

COT Dimensions

A modern-day Sprint Cup COT must have the following dimensions: 198.5 inches long, 74 inches wide, 53.5 inches tall, and a total weight of 3,450 pounds.

Front-runner Dale Earnhardt Jr. wins the 2008 Budweiser Shootout.

5 Start Your Engines!

The Daytona 500 is about more than just the big race. Two weeks of events, called Speedweeks, lead up to the main event. Hundreds of thousands of fans flock to the track for the festivities.

Since 1979 the week before the Daytona 500 has kicked off with the Saturday-night Budweiser Shootout. This 175-mile race is an all-star race. Only past shootout winners and the drivers who earned a pole position (first starting position) in the previous year take part.

Prepare to Qualify

The following day (Sunday) is qualifying day, also known as Pole Day. On this day, the need for speed is behind every decision. Crew members dig through toolboxes and crawl under cars. They work from checklists that are usually five to eight pages long. They make the changes needed for the cars to slice through the air and achieve top speeds for two laps. The race teams need a lot of preparation to create an aeropackage—a design that will cut through the air easily with the least amount of drag.

Testing, One, Two . . .

Testing is a scheduled practice time in which a race team tests new ideas and figures out how to get the car to run as fast as it can. To keep teams on equal footing, NASCAR has rules about testing. All the race teams are invited to six test days during the off-season on tracks picked by NASCAR. This rule keeps the big-money teams, which could afford to test more often, from having an advantage over smaller teams with tighter budgets.

Mark Martin holds the trophy he won for earning the pole position in the 2010 Daytona 500.

With the exception of water, all the fluids in the cars—from the motor oil to the transmission oil—are replaced with lighter and thinner fluids. To lighten the cars and reduce drag, the alternators, which generate electrical charges, are removed. They are replaced with high-voltage batteries. The cars are polished and waxed. The head pins, which hold the bodies to the cars, are pushed down. Even the tires are trimmed to reduce friction. Run your hand along an unused race tire, and you will feel little rubbery nubs. Before qualifying, team members shave the rubbery nubs from the tires. The front grills of the cars are taped. The crew runs ice water through the engines to keep them cool during the two-lap run.

From there, success is in the drivers' hands. Every car gets a warm-up lap, two qualifying laps, and a cool-down lap. It's a race against the clock, and the fastest time wins the pole position, the inside of the front row. The second-fastest time is awarded the outside pole position.

Together, the two cars make up the front row of the starting grid. They are also the only two cars whose starting positions are locked in on Pole Day.

Only 43 cars make up the starting lineup on race day. Qualifying for the Daytona 500 is unique to the sport. It can be grueling for even the most experienced teams and drivers. The first row (top two starting positions) is set on Pole Day. The rest of the field is set by a pair of qualifying races, called the Gatorade Duels. The top teams from the previous season are guaranteed to be among the 43 cars. Other teams must race their way into the Daytona 500.

Dueling at Daytona

The first Daytona 500 included both convertibles and hardtop cars. On February 20, 1959, two days before the race, a 100-mile convertible race took place. Immediately following that race, hardtop cars took to the course for their 100-mile race. These two races started the idea of twin qualifying races, a tradition that continues. However, the drivers of the convertibles felt as if they were being sucked out of their cars as they drove at such high speeds. The first Daytona 500 was the only one in which the convertibles competed.

Three cars run neck and neck in one of two Gatorade Duels before the 2010 Daytona 500.

"It's the rush of the Daytona 500. The culmination of months and months of hard work. All the sweat, the grease, and oil-stained clothes, the sleepless nights—it all leads to the moment when you roll off pit road for the pace laps of the greatest stock car race ever known to man, the Daytona 500. I've been fortunate enough to win at Daytona. I haven't won the 500, but I won the race in July. It's about having a great car, a great engine package, and winning that chess match in the closing laps. Daytona is a great track, and the Daytona 500 lives with history. I'm proud to be a part of it."

—John Andretti

Race Day

The prerace atmosphere is electrifying. Parachute teams trail colorful smoke as they land on the infield grass. Fireworks pop and crackle, leaving trails of glitter in the Florida sky. American flags flap in the ocean breeze to the sounds of "This Is My Country" and "America the Beautiful." The gritty mixture of rubber, gasoline, and motor oil clings to the air. Thousands of fans cluster on the track's sloped surface, cheering or jeering as drivers are introduced.

Fans look on during a very patriotic prerace show.

Fighter jets soar overhead. Race officials, race teams, drivers, and fans bow their heads in prayer. After the national anthem, the drivers climb into their cars. When the famous command—Gentlemen, start your engines!—is given, the ground shakes with the roar of the 43 engines.

The parade lap goes by. Drivers weave back and forth, heating up their tires. They go by a second time, in single file, following the pace car. This allows them to check their tachometers to gauge the Daytona maximum pit speed of 55 miles per hour. The pace car pulls off the track. The green flag drops, and the race is on.

The Daytona Draft

The cars jostle for position, buzzing around the track like a pack of angry hornets. It's a high-speed, bumper-to-bumper game of follow the leader.

Above: Jeff Gordon, *center stage*, greets fans before the start of the 2008 race. *Below:* The green flag drops, signaling the start of the Daytona 500.

The Quest for the Sprint Cup

The Daytona 500 is NASCAR's biggest race, but it's just the first race in a long season. The Sprint Cup season stretches over a 10-month, 36-race schedule. The first 26 races of the season are known as the Race for the Chase. The last 10 races are called the Chase for the Cup.

Drivers earn points for each race, according to their finish. The first-place driver earns 185 points. Second place gets 170, and the point totals diminish from there, with last place receiving 34 points. Five bonus points are awarded to any driver who leads a lap during the race. The driver who leads the most laps gets an additional five bonus points.

The top 12 drivers in points after the first 26 races qualify to race for the championship. All 12 drivers have their point totals set at 5,000. They receive an additional 10 points for every victory they scored during the regular season. The race for the Sprint Cup is on, and only one of the 12 will be driving away with the NASCAR Sprint Cup title at the end of the season.

Cars follow one another closely for a reason. As a stock car travels, it punches a hole in the air, creating a vacuum (space with little air) behind it. A car following with its nose close to another car's bumper faces less drag. This is called the draft. Drivers have learned that they can let off the gas without losing any speed when they're in the draft. Then, when they're ready to pass, the driver can slingshot past the competition.

Richard Petty was one of the first drivers to discover the draft. He later recalled his experience. "It was the first Daytona in 1959," he said. "I was a young kid. I didn't know anything, so I had a very open mind. I was taking in everything. Coming off of the second corner on the very last lap of the hundred-miler [duel race], I pulled out, passed some cars, and thought to myself, 'that was easy.' Coming off the fourth turn, they caught my draft and passed me. At first nobody knew what was happening or what it was. But right then, I figured out how to pass, and that was my introduction to the drafting deal."

The restrictor plates used at Daytona—and the reduced horsepower that comes with them—make the draft essential. A driver who leaves the draft without enough

Jimmy Johnson (No. 48) and Michael Waltrip (No. 55) lead the pack at the start of the 2008 Daytona 500. The cars will stay closely bunched, drafting, throughout the race. Cars that fall out of the draft will quickly fall behind.

momentum or who misjudges the timing of the move can be left in "dirty air." It's called being "hung out to dry," and it can be like putting on the brakes. The draft can be a driver's best friend or worst enemy.

It's the Pits

Richard Petty won the Daytona 500 in 1981, even though he didn't have the fastest car. "Bobby Allison had the fastest car that day," Petty said.

Follow the Leader

Ed Pimm was a rookie (first-year) driver at the 1988 Daytona 500. He remembers his first encounter with the Intimidator, Dale Earnhardt. During a practice run, the black No. 3 pulled alongside Pimm. Earnhardt pointed his finger. He was signaling Pimm to follow him. Pimm got in line, with Cale Yarborough ducking in behind him, to form a three-car train. The threesome did a few laps around the racing groove (the part of the track where the cars handle best). The two veterans were showing the rookie how to work the Daytona draft. After the session, Earnhardt pulled alongside of Pimm's car once again, this time signaling a thumbs-up.

Richard Petty, driving his No. 43 Buick, sees the checkered flag at the end of the 1981 Daytona 500.

"Near the end of the race, Allison ducked into the pits for tires and fuel, and everybody followed his lead. My crew chief, Dale Inman, got to thinking. He figured if we did the same thing as everybody else, we couldn't outrun the others. Inman kept me out a couple of extra laps and had me come in the pits for one can of gas. When I went back out on the track I had a three- to four-second lead because I had spent less time stopped. That day I didn't have the quickest car, but I had the quickest-thinking pit crew."

Petty's story shows the importance of a good pit crew. A successful stock car team runs like a fine-tuned piece of machinery. The drivers get most of the glory. But the pit crew, also known as the "over the wall gang," is one of the gears that drive a winning race team.

Pit stops are a race within a race. Positions on the track can be lost or gained by fractions of seconds spent in the pits. Seven team members perch on the wall, equipped with air guns, tires, gas, and a jack. They leap into action when the car comes to a stop. For a four-tire stop, they have to change four tires, add fuel, and make adjustments to the car, all in as little as 13 seconds.

The jackman, tire changers, and tire carriers dash to the right side of the car. The high-pitched whines of the air guns sound as five lug nuts are loosened on each wheel. The jackman cranks the right side of the car into the air. The old tire comes off, and the new one goes on. The air guns scream again, this time tightening the lug nuts. Meanwhile, the old tires go safely over the wall. The tire crew darts to the left side to repeat the drill. Old rubber is exchanged for new rubber in a flash.

Pit crew members service a car during the race.

At the same time, the gas man heaves the 85-pound gas can to the rear of the car while the catch can man plugs the valve into the back of the car. The catch can releases air out of the fuel cell to increase the flow of gas into the car. He knows the tank is full when fuel, not air, flows into the small catch can. When that happens, he raises his hand to signal that the car is fully fueled. A tear-off is removed to clean the windshield, and adjustments are made to the car. When the stop is complete, the

A Sticky Situation

There is no time for falling down on the job since race teams rely on speed on race day. When the car stops in the pit box, a fine brake dust falls from the hot brakes onto the pit road. This creates a slippery surface. Before the race, teams prepare the pit box by sweeping the area. After it is well swept, they take up to 14 cans of soda, shake them up, and spray the blacktop of the pit stall. This creates a sticky surface, much like a movie theater floor. The treated surface gives the team members the grip they need as they service the car.

The Harley J. Earl Daytona 500 Trophy

The Daytona 500 winner takes home one of the most prized possessions in auto racing, the Harley J. Earl Daytona 500 Trophy. The name of every Daytona 500 winner is inscribed onto the face of the trophy, along with the make of the winning car and the duration of the race.

Harley J. Earl was vice president of design for General Motors, the second national commissioner of NASCAR, and a friend of Bill France. He is the father of the Corvette and developed the Firebird concept car for General Motors. A sterling silver model of the Firebird, which performed on the beach in 1956, is the crowning feature of the trophy. A replica of the trophy is presented to the winner of the Daytona 500. In addition, the winning car is displayed for one year at Daytona USA, a museum and gallery next to the track.

driver races out of the pit stall, tires screeching.

To do all of this in 13 seconds takes a lot of preparation. Just as football and basketball teams must practice together, so must pit crews. They perform drills to sharpen footwork, speed, and accuracy. Weight training and fitness routines also help keep them on top of their game. The reward for all of this hard work is a well-orchestrated team and hopes for a trip to victory lane.

The Checkered Flag

The final laps of the Daytona 500 are frantic. The cars spread out in three or more lanes, battling for position. The leader often has to shift from lane to lane, trying to block all challengers. When the cars come out of the final turn, it's one last sprint down the front stretch. Only one driver can take the checkered flag and claim victory in the Great American Race.

For the newly crowned Daytona 500 champion, the celebration

Ryan Newman celebrates his victory in the 2008 Daytona 500 by doing burnouts under a sky filled with fireworks.

is just beginning. The winning driver usually shows off for the fans. He may do doughnuts (tight, full-circle turns in which the rear wheels skid along the pavement, leaving a doughnut-shaped mark) on the infield grass between the front stretch and pit row. Or he might do burnouts, spinning the car's tires on the pavement and creating a billowing cloud of smoke.

From there, it's off to victory lane. There the winning team and their families exchange backslaps, high fives, and bear hugs. Fireworks pop and confetti rains down on the celebration. The team is presented with the Harley J. Earl Daytona 500 Trophy, which they hoist high in the air.

The rest of the teams pack up their gear and head out. They'll have to wait another year before they get their next chance to win the Great American Race.

Special Feature:
BEHIND THE WHEEL WITH JOHN ANDRETTI

"I feather the throttle, reining in my rumbling race car behind the Corvette pace car traveling at speeds of nearly 90 miles per hour. For a powerful stock car, the pace lap is nearly a dull sleep. My thoughts wander. We are taking the second pace lap. I need to focus. I need to concentrate. It's almost like a different world once I put my helmet on. Like my wife Nancy says, I need to go to "Racer's Planet."

My spotter, my second set of eyes, is perched high above the speedway. He reminds me to check my pit road speed and to tighten my seat belts. My crew chief radios into my helmet, giving me final directions and wishing the team luck. I pull down on my straps and radio in one last time before the green drops. "Guys, you did a great job this past month. I know it's

A member of Andretti's crew helps fastens Andretti's window before a race.

a lot of hard work and dedication for this one race, but it's a big one. I just want to say 'thanks' for all your efforts. I'm going to do my best behind the wheel."

I shift my focus on the next 200 laps, 500 miles of the soon-to-be bumper-to-bumper 200 mile-per-hour chess match of guts and will. The green flag waves, and for the fans in the stands, it's 43 cars roaring to life like a pack of lions. The noise around me accelerates with the car. The car shakes, but it's gentle. It's like I'm crawling on the floor preparing for a full sprint. I'm excited but need to stay relaxed. I stay loose, but I'm totally focused on the cars in front.

I'm pushing the car through its paces from first to second gear. The car is on its way to fourth gear, and I'm pushing the restrictor-plated engine to its limits. I hit the banking in the first turn as my car continues to accelerate. My body weight shifts to the left. The tires grip to the track, and it's like a big hand is pushing my car through the turns. My head rests to the right, sitting on a padded bar to keep it from going out the right-side window. I'm on my first lap of turns into a grueling mind game of car and track position.

Throughout the day, the draft rockets me from the back to the front in a matter of a straightaway. It seems I'm not in one spot for more than a lap or so. The draft shuffles the cars quickly, and guys are always making moves. I try my best to stay in a line during the early and middle stages of the race. There is no need to take chances until the last 50 laps. They are always some of the toughest. I stay focused in an environment of lightning-fast moves and split-second decisions. The car smells of burning rubber, gas, and other fumes. It's like walking into a mechanic shop at 200 miles per hour.

It's hot, blazing hot. The Daytona sun is beating down, and the asphalt is soaking it in like a sponge. The car is all metal, and soon my helmet is full of sweat. My body is trying to cool itself, but my fire suit, gloves, helmet, and shoes trap the heat. There is no place for it to escape, and soon sweat covers my entire body. My cooling system comes through my helmet and does its best to blow cooler air. It's the only relief. Still, I'm inches away from 42 other cars going nearly 200 miles per hour. The car is still rumbling from its horsepower. I'm concentrating. I'm fighting to look through the oil and other liquids that nearly cover my windshield. The car is vibrating gently, but not enough to limit me. I keep pushing through.

Now it's the last lap. I take the white flag, and I know it's the last time around Daytona after a long winter preparing. There are cars in front of me, behind me, to the right, and to the left. I'm surrounded, but this time, the patience is gone. It's time to go, and I'm fighting to stick my car into the slightest of holes I see. It's breathtaking as I thread the needle at 200 miles per hour. I can go three-wide at Daytona, but it's hard. I'm in a tunnel of cars, and I keep my foot down.

I'm hearing noises that weren't there at the beginning of the race. The engine is whining, and there are knocks and bumps that I'm not sure where they are coming from. I'm still pushing. It's my one shot to get the most out of this lap. I can gain multiple positions. My spotter is telling me what line is moving. I pick the line that I feel is best and press forward. I'm coming off the final turn. I'm not holding my breath, but it feels like it. In front of me, cars fan out trying to get that last push of air. I put my car in the best spot and cross the line underneath the checkered flag. I breathe easier as I decelerate the car. It's been a grueling day. I'm mentally and physically drained. I'm relieved it's over but eager to get to the next track. I always want to do better than the last race. For now, I'm back from Racer's Planet. It was a good trip.

FLAGS OF NASCAR

A variety of colored flags are waved to control the race. Each color sends a different message to the drivers.

 GREEN—A green flag means that the track is clear and the drivers may proceed at speed. A green flag signals the beginning of the race and is used in restarts.

 YELLOW—This flag warns the drivers of a caution. The cars must slow down and hold position behind the pace car. A yellow flag can signal an accident, debris on the track, or weather-related issues.

BLACK—This flag instructs a driver to pit, often in response to a rules violation.

 **WHITE**—This flag waves on the final lap of the race.

RED—This flag tells drivers that the track is unsafe. Cars must go to a set location and stop. In addition, NASCAR reserves the right to throw a red flag in the closing laps of a race to make sure that an event does not end under a caution period. Teams are not allowed to work on or repair their cars while the red flag is displayed.

 CHECKERED—This flag signals the end of the race. The winning car "takes the checkered flag" as it crosses the finish line.

NASCAR GLOSSARY AND SLANG

aeropackage: a design that will cut through the air easily with the least amount of drag

alternator: a part that powers the car's electronic gear and charges the battery while the engine is running

backstretch: the straightaway on the back side of the racetrack, usually opposite the start/finish line

banking: the sloping of a racetrack, particularly at a curve or a corner, from the apron (very bottom of the track) or inside of the track to the outside wall. The degree of banking refers to the height of a racetrack's slope at the outside edge. On oval tracks, the corners are often tilted inward to provide faster speeds.

block: the metal casing of an engine. The block contains the cylinder heads, crankcase, engine mounts, and other major parts.

caution: a period of the race in which the cars slow down to follow a pace car and cannot pass one another on the track due to an unsafe driving condition. A caution period is denoted by a yellow flag.

cylinder heads: the part above the cylinders on the top of the engine's block. The cylinder heads contain the valves and ports that distribute the fuel/air mixture and the exhaust.

deck lid: the rear trunk area of a race car

dirty air: the air alongside and behind any car

draft: the aerodynamic effect that allows two or more cars traveling nose to tail to run faster than a single car

drag: air resistance

dynamometer: a machine that measures an engine's horsepower and other characteristics

floor pan: the bottom metal structure of a race car's interior

front stretch: the straightaway located on the front part of the track. It usually includes the start/finish line.

fuel cell: a metal box that contains a flexible, tear-resistant bladder and foam baffling. It holds the race car's supply of gasoline.

greenhouse: the inside of the car between the front windshield and the rear windshield

groove: the fastest line a car can take around the track. It is visible by the blackened pavement created by the cars using it. Some tracks have one racing groove. Other tracks, such as Daytona, have multiple racing grooves.

handling: a term to describe a race car's performance while racing, qualifying, or practicing. How a car "handles" is determined by its tires, suspension, geometry, aerodynamics, and other factors.

HANS: a head and neck restraint system that protects drivers during crashes

horsepower: a unit used to measure engine power. One horsepower is the estimated power needed to lift 33,000 pounds one foot per minute, roughly equated with a horse's strength.

lapped car: a car that has completed at least one lap fewer than the leader

loose: a handling condition that occurs when a car's rear tires lose grip with the track. A loose setup is sometimes referred to as hanging it out.

manifold: a pipe that distributes air inside an engine. There are two manifolds—an intake and an exhaust. The air and fuel mixture travels through the intake manifold into the cylinders, and the exhaust manifold directs the spent air-fuel mixture out.

piston: an engine part that moves rapidly up and down to ignite fuel and power the engine

pit road: the area, usually located along the front straightaway, where pit crews service the cars

pit stall: an area along a pit road that is designated for a particular team's use

pole position: the starting position awarded to the fastest qualifier. The driver gets to pick the inside or the outside of the front row.

radiator: a part that cools the engine by passing liquid coolant through the engine block

restrictor plate: an aluminum plate with four holes drilled in it. It is placed between the base of the carburetor and the engine's intake manifold. The plate's design reduces the flow of air and fuel into the engine's combustion chamber, thereby decreasing horsepower and speed.

rod: an engine part that connects the piston to the crankshaft

slingshot: to pass a car by using the draft

Sprint Cup: the world's premier stock car racing series sanctioned by NASCAR. It is named for the current sponsor of the series. The term also refers to the trophy given to the series champion each season.

stock car: a racing machine with a full body. Stock cars resemble common passenger cars but are specially built for racing.

superspeedway: an oval track at least one mile long

tachometer: an instrument that measures the engine's rpms

tight: a handling condition that occurs when a car's front tires lose grip with the track

trading paint: slang for when two cars come in contact with each other

tri-oval: a track that has a D-shape rather than a perfect oval

SOURCE NOTES

5   *Daytona 500—50 Years: The Great American Race*, DVD, directed by John M. Best (Charlotte, NC: NASCAR Media Group, 2008).

5   "Daytona 500 History," Daytona International Speedway, 2010, http://www.aytonainternationalspeedway .com/News/DAYTONA-500-History.aspx (June 20, 2010).

13   Richard Petty, telephone interview with the author, April 14, 2010.

13   *NASCAR: The Imax Experience*, DVD, directed by Simon Wincher (Burbank, CA: Warner Bros. Pictures, 2004).

15   Duane Falk, *The Daytona 500: The Great American Race* (New York: Metro Books, 2002), 36.

16   Petty interview.

16   Tom Higgins, *NASCAR Greatest Races: The 25 Most Thrilling Races in NASCAR History* (New York: Harper Entertainment, 1999), 17.

16–17   Ibid.

19   *Daytona 500—50 Years: The Great American Race*.

19   Ibid.

23   Ibid.

24   Bob Zeller, *Daytona 500: An Official History* (Phoenix: David Bull Publishing, 2002), 106.

27   Higgins, *NASCAR Greatest Races*, 44.

27   Ibid.

28   A. R. McHugh, *Dale Earnhardt* (Chanhassen, MN: Child's World, 2001), 17.

28   Ibid.

29   Higgins, *NASCAR Greatest Races*, 131.

30   Editors of *NASCAR Scene, Thunder and Glory: The 25 Most Memorable Races in NASCAR Winston Cup History* (Chicago: Triumph Books, 2004), 27.

31   Ibid.

32   Jamie McMurray, interview with the author, March 23, 2010.

33   Ibid.

33   Ibid.

38   Tony Santanicola, interview with the author, February 16, 2007.

46   John Andretti, interview with the author, February 16, 2007.

48   Petty interview.

49–50   Ibid.

FURTHER READING

Books

Buckley, James, Jr. *NASCAR*. New York: DK Publishing, 2005.

Editors of *NASCAR Scene. Thunder and Glory: The 25 Most Memorable Races in NASCAR Winston Cup History*. Chicago: Triumph Books, 2004.

Falk, Duane. *The Daytona 500: The Great American Race*. New York: Metro Books, 2002.

Higgins, Tom. *NASCAR Greatest Races: The 25 Most Thrilling Races in NASCAR History*. New York: Harper Entertainment, 1999.

Hinton, Ed. *Daytona—from the Birth of Speed to the Death of the Man in Black*. New York: Warner Books, 2001.

Poole, David, and Jim McLaurin. *Then Junior Said to Jeff . . . the Best NASCAR Stories Ever Told*. Chicago: Triumph Books, 2006.

Savage, Jeff. *Dale Earnhardt Jr.* Minneapolis: Lerner Publications Company, 2009.

———. *Danica Patrick*. Minneapolis: Lerner Publications Company, 2011.

———. *Jeff Gordon*. Minneapolis: Lerner Publications Company, 2003.

Stewart, Mark, and Mike Kennedy. The Science of NASCAR series. Minneapolis: Lerner Publications Company, 2008.

Zeller, Bob. *Daytona 500: An Official History*. Phoenix: David Bull Publishing, 2002.

Websites

Daytona International Speedway   http://www.daytonainternationalspeedway.com
The home page of Daytona International Speedway features lots of information about the track that hosts the Great American Race. Check out track maps, seating charts, ticket information, and tips for fans making the trip to the track.

NASCAR   http://www.nascar.com
The official site of NASCAR has all the latest news on the Sprint Cup series, including the Daytona 500. Check the site for past results, points standings, driver biographies, and much more.

Sports Illustrated—Racing   http://sportsillustrated.cnn.com/racing
SI.com's racing page highlights all forms of auto racing, including the Sprint Cup and the Daytona 500. The site features the latest news in racing, stories on drivers, statistics, and more.

INDEX

Page numbers in italics refer to illustrations.

Allison, Bobby, 15, 24, 27, *27*, 33, 39, 49–50
Allison, Davey, 27, *27*
Allison, Donnie, 23–24, *23–24*
Andretti, John, 46, *54–55*, 55–56
Andretti, Mario, 5, 20, *20*

Beauchamp, Johnny, 16, *17*
Budweiser Shootout, *42*, 43

Campbell, Malcolm, 9–10, *9*
Car of Tomorrow (COT), 26, 35
Croker, Frank, 8

Daytona Beach International Speedway, 14–15, *15*
draft, 47–49, 55

Earl, Harley J., 52
Earnhardt, Dale, 24, 28–29, *28–29*, 30–31, 49
Earnhardt, Dale, Jr., 32, *32*, 42
Elliott, Bill, 25, *25*, 33, 39

France, "Big Bill," 10–12, *10*, 14, 16, 31, 52

Gatorade Duels, 45, *45*
Gordon, Jeff, 5, 33, *47*
Guthrie, Janet, 22

Hamilton, Pete, 36
HANS, 31, 35
Harley J. Earl Daytona 500 Trophy, 26, 52–53

Inman, Dale, 50

Jarrett, Dale, 33
Jarrett, Ned, 19
Johnson, Jimmy, *49*
Johnson, Junior, 26

Labonte, Bobby, 28
Lexan, 36–37
Lloyd, Saxton, 14
Lorenzen, Fred, 19
Lund, DeWayne "Tiny," 18–19, *19*

Martin, Mark, *44*
Martin, Sterling, 33
Mast, Rick, 28
Mayfield, Jeremy, 28
McMurray, Jamie, 32–33, *32–33*

National Championship Beach and Road Race, 10
Newman, Ryan, *41*, 53

Olds, Ransom E., 7
Ormond Challenge Cup, 7

Panch, Marvin, 18–19, *18*
parade lap, 47
Pearson, David, 21–22, *21–22*
Petty, Lee, 13, 16, *17*
Petty, Richard, 13, 16, 21–22, *21–22*, 23–24, 26, *26*, 33, 48–50, *50*
photo finish, 16–17
Pimm, Ed, 49
pit crew, 50–52

Pole Day, 43, 45
pole position, 44

Raoul, Alexander, 8
restrictor plates, 26, 39–40, 48
Riggs, Scott, *36*
Robinson, Shawna, 22

Santanicola, Tony, 38
Schrader, Ken, 30
Segrave, Henry, 8, *8*
Smith, Louise, 22
Speedweeks, 5, 8, 43
Sprint Cup Series, 5, 35, 40, 48
Squier, Ken, 15, 23

tachometer, 37, 47
Thomas, H. T., 7
Thompson, Jimmy, 15

Vogt, Red, 12

Waltrip, Darrell, 24, 27, 30
Waltrip, Michael, 30–31, *31*, 33, *38, 49*
Weatherly, Joe, 16, *17*
Winter Speed Carnival, 8
Winton, Alex, 7
Wood, Glen, 18–19
Wood, Leonard, 18–19

Yarborough, Cale, *23–24*, 23–25, 33, 49

ABOUT THE AUTHOR

Nancy Roe Pimm married her childhood sweetheart, Ed Pimm, and the couple traveled across the country while he pursued a career in auto racing. Nancy worked in the pit box timing and scoring while Ed competed in both the NASCAR and the Indy Car Series, driving in both the Indy 500 and the Daytona 500. She gives the reader an inside look into the exciting world of auto racing in her books *The Daytona 500: The Thrill and Thunder of the Great American Race* and *The Indy 500: The Inside Track.* Nancy and Ed reside in Plain City, Ohio. They have three daughters, Allison, Lindsay, and Carli, a son-in-law Rusty Simkins, and a grandson named Tommy.

Photo Acknowledgments

The images in this book are used with the permission of: © Chris Graythen/Getty Images, p. 4; © Bettmann/CORBIS, pp. 6, 9; © iStockphoto.com/ktsimage, pp. 8 (top), 11 (bottom), 13, 15 (bottom), 22 (bottom), 24 (bottom), 26 (background), 31 (bottom), 33 (top), 35 (bottom), 36 (bottom), 37, 38 (bottom), 39, 44 (top), 45 (top), 48, 49 (bottom), 51 (bottom), 52 (background); © Southern Photo Archives/Alamy, p. 8 (bottom); AP Photo, pp. 10, 18, 20 (bottom), 22 (top); © RacingOne/ISC Archives/Getty Images, pp. 11 (top), 12, 15 (top), 17, 20 (top), 21, 27; AP Photo/James P. Kerlin, p. 19; © Ric Feld/St. Petersburg Times/ZUMA Press, p. 23; AP Photo/Ric Feld, p. 24 (top); AP Photo/Kathy Willens, p. 25; © Kevin Kane/WireImage/Getty Images, p. 26; AP Photo/Phil Coale, p. 28; AP Photo/Chris O'Meara, pp. 29, 38 (top); © Jamie Squire/Allsport/Getty Images, p. 30; © Robert Laberge/Allsport/Getty Images, pp. 31 (top), 55; AP Photo/David Graham, pp. 32, 40, 42, 47 (top); AP Photo/John Raoux, p. 33 (bottom); © Cameras in Action Photography, pp. 35 (top), 36 (top), 51 (top); AP Photo/Lynne Sladky, p. 41; AP Photo/John Bazemore, p. 44 (bottom); © Stephen A. Acre/ASP/Icon SMI, p. 45 (bottom); © Jamie Squire/Getty Images for NASCAR, p. 46; AP Photo/Jamie Squire, Pool, pp. 47 (bottom), 53, 57 (bottom); © George Tiedemann/GT Images/CORBIS, p. 49 (top); AP Photo/Wright, p. 50; © John Harrelson/Getty Images for NASCAR, p. 52; © John Andretti, p. 54; © iStockphoto.com/Joachim Angeltun, p. 57 (top).

Front Cover: © George Tiedemann/GT Images/CORBIS. Front Cover Flap: © Kevin Kane/WireImage/Getty Images (top), © Allen Kee/WireImage/Getty Images (bottom).

MAY 2 0 2011